HUGGA SUPERHEROES

SPARK YOUR CHILD'S IMAGINATION WITH 5 EASY-TO-CROCHET CHARACTERS!

These sweet superheroes will share their capes, masks, shield, and even a tiara with any child. Watch the everyday Anton, Charles, Marvin, Patty, and Violet transform into ATOMIC FLYER, CRIMSON DEFENDER, MEGA BOY, POWERFUL PRINCESS, and VALIANT HEART. Measuring 15 inches tall seated, they are just the right size to be the greatest hero for your child.

LEISURE ARTS, INC. • Maumelle, Arkansas

ANTON

ATOMIC FLYER

 **EASY**

SHOPPING LIST

Yarn (Super Bulky Weight)
[3.5 ounces, 108 yards
(100 grams, 99 meters) per skein**]**:

- ☐ Orange - 3 skeins
- ☐ White - 2 skeins
- ☐ Brown - 1 skein
- ☐ Black - 1 skein
- ☐ Gold - small amount

Crochet Hook

- ☐ Size J (6 mm)

    or size needed for gauge

Additional Supplies

- ☐ Safety pins
- ☐ Yarn needle
- ☐ 15 mm Safety eyes - 2
- ☐ Polyester fiberfill - 12 ounces (340 grams)

Finished Size: ~15" (38 cm) tall (seated)

GAUGE INFORMATION

10 sc and 12 rows/rnds = 4" (10 cm)

Gauge Swatch: 4" (10 cm) square
With Brown, ch 11.

Row 1: Sc in second ch from hook and in each ch across: 10 sc.

Rows 2-12: Ch 1, turn; sc in each sc across.
Finish off.

STITCH GUIDE

SINGLE CROCHET 2 TOGETHER
  (abbreviated sc2tog)

Pull up a loop in each of next 2 sc, YO and draw through all 3 loops on hook **(counts as one sc)**.

HAT
Body

Rnd 1 (Right side)**:** With Orange, ch 2, 8 sc in second ch from hook; do **not** join, place marker to indicate beginning of rnd *(see Markers, page 45)*.

Note: Loop a short piece of yarn around any stitch to mark Rnd 1 as **right** side.

Rnd 2: 2 Sc in each sc around: 16 sc.

Rnd 3: (Sc in next sc, 2 sc in next sc) around: 24 sc.

Rnd 4: (Sc in next 2 sc, 2 sc in next sc) around: 32 sc.

Rnd 5: (Sc in next 3 sc, 2 sc in next sc) around: 40 sc.

Rnd 6: (Sc in next 4 sc, 2 sc in next sc) around: 48 sc.

Rnds 7-10: Sc in each sc around.

Rnd 11: Sc in each sc around; with Black, slip st in next sc *(Fig. 4, page 46)*, drop Orange.

Rnd 12: Ch 1, sc in same st as slip st and in each sc around; with Orange, join with slip st to first sc, drop Black.

Rnd 13: With Orange, ch 1, sc in same st as joining and in each sc around; with Black, join with slip st to first sc, drop Orange.

Rnd 14: With Black, ch 1, sc in same st as joining and in each sc around; with Orange, join with slip st to first sc, cut Black.

Rnd 15: With Orange, ch 1, sc in same st as joining and in each sc around; join with slip st to first sc, finish off leaving a long end for sewing.

First Flap

Row 1: With **right** side facing, skip next 10 sc on Rnd 15 from joining and join Orange with sc in next sc *(see Joining With Sc, page 45)*; sc in next 4 sc, leave remaining sc unworked: 5 sc.

Rows 2 and 3: Ch 1, turn; sc in each sc across.

Row 4: Turn; beginning in first sc, sc2tog, sc in next sc, sc2tog: 3 sc.

Row 5: Turn; beginning in first sc, sc2tog, beginning in last sc2tog, sc2tog; finish off: 2 sc.

Second Flap

Row 1: With **right** side facing, skip next 19 sc on Rnd 15 from First Flap and join Orange with sc in next sc; sc in next 4 sc, leave remaining sc unworked: 5 sc.

Rows 2 and 3: Ch 1, turn; sc in each sc across.

Row 4: Turn; beginning in first sc, sc2tog, sc in next sc, sc2tog: 3 sc.

Row 5: Turn; beginning in first sc, sc2tog, beginning in last sc2tog, sc2tog; finish off: 2 sc.

Trim

With **right** side facing, join Black with sc in same st as joining on Rnd 15; sc in each sc and in end of each row around; join with slip st to first sc, finish off.

HEAD & BODY

Rnd 1 (Right side)**:** With Brown and beginning at top of Head, ch 2, 8 sc in second ch from hook; do **not** join, place marker to indicate beginning of rnd.

Note: Mark Rnd 1 as **right** side.

Rnd 2: 2 Sc in each sc around: 16 sc.

Rnd 3: (Sc in next sc, 2 sc in next sc) around: 24 sc.

Rnd 4: (Sc in next 2 sc, 2 sc in next sc) around: 32 sc.

Rnd 5: (Sc in next 3 sc, 2 sc in next sc) around: 40 sc.

Rnd 6: (Sc in next 4 sc, 2 sc in next sc) around: 48 sc.

Rnds 7-15: Sc in each sc around.

Rnd 16: (Sc in next 4 sc, sc2tog) around: 40 sc.

Rnd 17: Sc in each sc around.

Rnd 18: (Sc in next 3 sc, sc2tog) around: 32 sc.

Rnd 19: (Sc in next 2 sc, sc2tog) around; slip loop from hook onto a safety pin to prevent Head from unraveling while attaching eyes, nose, and Hat: 24 sc.

Attach safety eyes on Rnd 12 of Head, spacing them 6 sc apart.

Using photo, page 4, as a guide for placement and satin stitch *(Fig. 7, page 46)*, add Brown nose 2 rnds below eyes.

Stuff Head firmly with polyester fiberfill. Using photo, page 4, as a guide for placement, place Hat on Head angling toward the back; using safety pins, pin Hat to Head; remove polyester fiberfill.

Using long end, sew Hat to Head, leaving flaps unsewn.
Remove safety pins.

Rnd 20: Slip loop from safety pin onto crochet hook; (sc2tog, sc in next sc) around: 16 sc.

Rnd 21: (Sc in next sc, 2 sc in next sc) around: 24 sc.

Rnd 22: (Sc in next 2 sc, 2 sc in next sc) around: 32 sc.

Rnd 23: Sc in each sc around; slip st in next sc, finish off.

Rnd 24: With **right** side facing, join White with sc in same st as slip st; sc in next 2 sc, 2 sc in next sc, (sc in next 3 sc, 2 sc in next sc) around; join with slip st to first sc: 40 sc.

Rnd 25: Ch 1, sc in same st as joining and in each sc around; do **not** join, place marker to indicate beginning of rnd.

Rnd 26: Sc in each sc around.

Rnd 27: (Sc in next 4 sc, 2 sc in next sc) around: 48 sc.

Rnds 28-36: Sc in each sc around.

Slip st in next sc, finish off.

Using photo, page 3, as a guide for placement and satin stitch, add one Black accent line to front of Body on Rnd 25 working around 6 sc. Add second accent line on Rnd 27 working around 7 sc.

Rnd 37: With **right** side facing, join Orange with sc in same st as slip st; sc in each sc around; join with slip st to first sc.

Rnd 38: Ch 1, sc in same st as joining and in each sc around; do **not** join, place marker to indicate beginning of rnd.

Rnds 39-42: Sc in each sc around.

Rnd 43: (Sc2tog, sc in next 4 sc) around: 40 sc.

Rnd 44: (Sc2tog, sc in next 3 sc) around: 32 sc.

Rnd 45: (Sc2tog, sc in next 2 sc) around: 24 sc.

Stuff Head & Body with polyester fiberfill.

Rnd 46: (Sc2tog, sc in next sc) around: 16 sc.

Rnd 47: Sc2tog around: 8 sc.

Rnd 48: Sc in each sc around; slip st in next sc, finish off leaving a long end for sewing.

Thread yarn needle with long end and weave needle through sts on Rnd 48 *(Fig. 5, page 46)*; pull **tightly** to close hole and secure end.

ARM (Make 2)

Rnd 1 (Right side)**:** With Brown, ch 2, 4 sc in second ch from hook; do **not** join, place marker to indicate beginning of rnd.

Note: Mark Rnd 1 as **right** side.

Rnd 2: 2 Sc in each sc around: 8 sc.

Rnd 3: (Sc in next sc, 2 sc in next sc) around: 12 sc.

Rnds 4-7: Sc in each sc around.

Slip st in next sc, finish off.

Rnd 8: With **right** side facing, join White with sc in same st as slip st; sc in each sc around; join with slip st to first sc.

Rnd 9: Ch 1, sc in same st as joining and in each sc around; do **not** join, place marker to indicate beginning of rnd.

Rnds 10-23: Sc in each sc around.

Slip st in next sc, finish off leaving a long end for sewing.

Stuff Arms with polyester fiberfill, leaving top unstuffed.

LEG (Make 2)

With White, ch 4.

Rnd 1 (Right side)**:** Sc in second ch from hook and in next ch, 4 sc in last ch; working in free loops of beginning ch *(Fig. 3b, page 45)*, sc in next ch, 3 sc in next ch; join with slip st to first sc: 10 sc.

Note: Mark Rnd 1 as **right** side.

Rnd 2: Ch 1, sc in same st as joining and in next sc, 2 sc in each of next 4 sc, sc in next 2 sc, 2 sc in each of last 2 sc; join with slip st to first sc: 16 sc.

Rnd 3: Ch 1, sc in same st as joining and in next 2 sc, 2 sc in next sc, (sc in next sc, 2 sc in next sc) 3 times, sc in next 3 sc, 2 sc in next sc, sc in next sc, 2 sc in last sc; join with slip st to Back Loop Only of first sc *(Fig. 2, page 45)*: 22 sc.

Rnd 4: Ch 1, sc in Back Loop Only of same st as joining and in each sc around; join with slip st to **both** loops of first sc.

Rnd 5: Ch 1, sc in same st as joining and in each sc around; join with slip st to first sc.

Rnd 6: Ch 1, sc in same st as joining and in next 2 sc, sc2tog (sc in next sc, sc2tog) 3 times, sc in each sc around; join with slip st to first sc: 18 sc.

Rnd 7: Ch 1, sc in same st as joining and in next sc, sc2tog 4 times, sc in each sc around; join with slip st to first sc: 14 sc.

Rnd 8: Ch 1, sc in same st as joining and in each sc around; join with slip st to first sc, finish off.

Rnd 9: With **right** side facing, join Black with sc in same st as joining; sc in each sc around; join with slip st to first sc, finish off.

Rnd 10: With **right** side facing, join Orange with sc in same st as joining; sc in each sc around; join with slip st to first sc.

Rnd 11: Ch 1, sc in same st as joining and in each sc around; do **not** join, place marker to indicate beginning of rnd.

Rnds 15-28: Sc in each sc around.

Slip st in next sc, finish off leaving a long end for sewing.

Stuff Legs with polyester fiberfill, leaving top unstuffed.

BELT

With Black, ch 48.

Row 1 (Right side)**:** Sc in back ridge of second ch from hook and each ch across *(Fig. 1, page 45)*; finish off leaving a long end for sewing: 47 sc.

Note: Mark Row 1 as **right** side.

BUCKLE

With Black, ch 5.

Row 1 (Right side)**:** Sc in back ridge of second ch from hook and each ch across: 4 sc.

Note: Mark Row 1 as **right** side.

Rows 2 and 3: Ch 1, turn; sc in each sc across.

Finish off.

Using photo, page 7, as a guide for placement and satin stitch, add gold accent to Buckle.

CAPE

With Orange, ch 22.

Row 1 (Right side)**:** Sc in back ridge of second ch from hook and each ch across: 21 sc.

Note: Mark Row 1 as **right** side.

Rows 2 and 3: Ch 1, turn; sc in each sc across.

Row 4: Ch 1, turn; sc in first 2 sc, 2 sc in next sc, (sc in next 2 sc, 2 sc in next sc) across: 28 sc.

Rows 5 and 6: Ch 1, turn; sc in each sc across.

Row 7: Ch 1, turn; sc in first 3 sc, 2 sc in next sc, (sc in next 3 sc, 2 sc in next sc) across: 35 sc.

Rows 8-35: Ch 1, turn; sc in each sc across.

Finish off.

Trim: With Black, ch 20 (**first tie made**); with **right** side facing, sc in end of Row 1 and in each row across to last row, skip last row; 3 sc in first sc, sc in each sc across to last sc, 3 sc in last sc; skip first row, sc in end of each row across, ch 20 (**second tie made**); finish off.

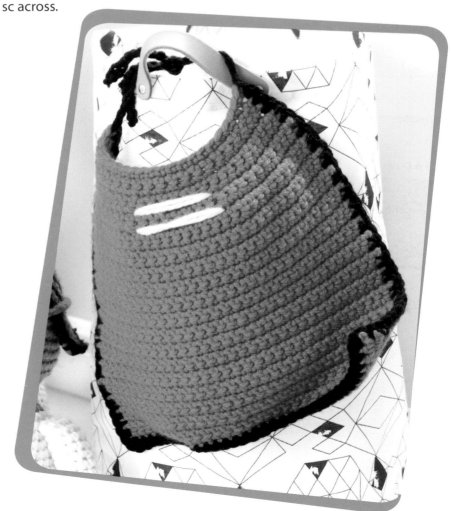

Using photo, page 8, as a guide for placement and satin stitch, add one White accent line on Row 5 working around 7 sc. Add second White accent line on Row 7 working around 8 sc.

MASK

With Orange, beginning at center between eyes, slip st around each eye; finish off leaving a long end for sewing.

With long end and using satin stitch, add bridge to Mask.

Ties

With **right** side facing, join Orange with slip st in slip st on one side of Mask; ch 29; finish off.

Repeat on opposite side.

Tie Ties in a bow.

ASSEMBLY

Using photo as a guide for placement, with **right** sides of all pieces facing and using long ends:

Sew Belt to Buckle; then sew Belt to Body.

Thumb: With **right** side facing, join Brown with slip st around post of sc on Rnd 6 of Arm; ch 3, slip st around post of sc on Rnd 7; finish off.

Repeat for second Arm.

Flatten Arms; then sew to Rnd 25 on each side of Body.

Flatten Legs; then sew to Rnds 44-48 on each side at bottom of Body.

Tie Cape around neck.

PATTY

POWERFUL PRINCESS

●●○○ EASY

SHOPPING LIST

Yarn (Super Bulky Weight)
[3.5 ounces, 108 yards
(100 grams, 99 meters) per skein]:

☐ Blue - 3 skeins

☐ Brown - 2 skeins

☐ Pink - 2 skeins

☐ Dark Brown - 1 skein

☐ Gold - 1 skein

☐ Black medium weight - small
amount (for eyelashes)

Crochet Hook

☐ Size J (6 mm)

or size needed for gauge

Additional Supplies

☐ Safety pins

☐ Yarn needle

☐ 15 mm Safety eyes - 2

☐ Polyester fiberfill - 12 ounces (340 grams)

Finished Size: 15" (38 cm) tall (seated)

GAUGE INFORMATION

10 sc and 12 rows/rnds = 4" (10 cm)

Gauge Swatch: 4" (10 cm) square
With Brown, ch 11.

Row 1: Sc in second ch from hook
and in each ch across: 10 sc.

Rows 2-12: Ch 1, turn; sc in each sc
across.

Finish off.

STITCH GUIDE

TREBLE CROCHET *(abbreviated tr)*

YO twice, insert hook in sc indicated,
YO and pull up a loop (4 loops on
hook), (YO and draw through 2 loops
on hook) 3 times.

SINGLE CROCHET 2 TOGETHER
  (abbreviated sc2tog)

Pull up a loop in each of next 2 sc,
YO and draw through all 3 loops on
hook (**counts as one sc**).

HAIR
Body

Rnd 1 (Right side)**:** With Dark Brown,
ch 2, 8 sc in second ch from hook;
do **not** join, place marker to indicate
beginning of rnd *(see Markers,
page 45)*.

Note: Loop a short piece of yarn
around any stitch to mark Rnd 1 as
right side.

Rnd 2: 2 Sc in each sc around: 16 sc.

Rnd 3: (Sc in next sc, 2 sc in next sc)
around: 24 sc.

Rnd 4: (Sc in next 2 sc, 2 sc in next sc)
around: 32 sc.

Rnd 5: (Sc in next 3 sc, 2 sc in next sc)
around: 40 sc.

Rnd 6: (Sc in next 4 sc, 2 sc in next sc)
around: 48 sc.

Rnds 7-11: Sc in each sc around.

Rnd 12: ★ Slip st in next sc, skip next
2 sc, 5 dc in next sc, skip next 2 sc;
repeat from ★ around; slip st in first
slip st, finish off leaving a long end
for sewing.

Spiral Curl (Make 14)
With Dark Brown, ch 13.

Row 1: 3 Sc in second ch from hook
and in each ch across; finish off
leaving a long end for sewing.

Thread yarn needle with one long
end, run needle through end of
7 Spiral Curls to form first pigtail; pull
to tighten and secure end.

Repeat with remaining 7 Spiral Curls
to form second pigtail.

HEAD & BODY

Rnd 1 (Right side): With Brown and beginning at top of Head, ch 2, 8 sc in second ch from hook; do **not** join, place marker to indicate beginning of rnd.

Note: Mark Rnd 1 as **right** side.

Rnd 2: 2 Sc in each sc around: 16 sc.

Rnd 3: (Sc in next sc, 2 sc in next sc) around: 24 sc.

Rnd 4: (Sc in next 2 sc, 2 sc in next sc) around: 32 sc.

Rnd 5: (Sc in next 3 sc, 2 sc in next sc) around: 40 sc.

Rnd 6: (Sc in next 4 sc, 2 sc in next sc) around: 48 sc.

Rnds 7-15: Sc in each sc around.

Rnd 16: (Sc in next 4 sc, sc2tog) around: 40 sc.

Rnd 17: Sc in each sc around.

Rnd 18: (Sc in next 3 sc, sc2tog) around: 32 sc.

Rnd 19: (Sc in next 2 sc, sc2tog) around; slip loop from hook onto a safety pin to prevent Head from unraveling while attaching eyes, nose, and Hair: 24 sc.

Attach safety eyes on Rnd 12 of Head, spacing them 6 sc apart.

Using photo as a guide for placement and satin stitch *(Fig. 7, page 46)*, add Brown nose 2 rnds below eyes and using straight stitch *(Fig. 6, page 46)* and medium weight Black, add eyelashes.

Stuff Head firmly with polyester fiberfill. Using photo as a guide for placement, place Hair Body on Head angling toward the back.
Place markers on each side of Head for placement of pigtails.
Pull ends of each Spiral Curl on pigtail through Body at marked sc; then secure ends. Repeat on opposite side.
Place Hair Body on Head angling toward the back. Using safety pins, pin Hair Body to Head; remove polyester fiberfill. Using long end, sew Hair Body to Head.
Remove safety pins.

Rnd 20: Slip loop from safety pin onto crochet hook; (sc2tog, sc in next sc) around: 16 sc.

Rnd 21: (Sc in next sc, 2 sc in next sc) around: 24 sc.

Rnd 22: (Sc in next 2 sc, 2 sc in next sc) around: 32 sc.

Rnd 23: Sc in each sc around; slip st in next sc, finish off.

Rnd 24: With **right** side facing, join Blue with sc in same st as slip st *(see Joining With Sc, page 45)*; sc in next 2 sc, 2 sc in next sc, (sc in next 3 sc, 2 sc in next sc) around; join with slip st to first sc: 40 sc.

Rnd 25: Ch 1, sc in same st as joining and in each sc around; do **not** join, place marker to indicate beginning of rnd.

Rnd 26: Sc in each sc around.

Rnd 27: (Sc in next 4 sc, 2 sc in next sc) around: 48 sc.

Rnds 28-36: Sc in each sc around.

Rnd 37: Sc in Back Loop Only of each sc around *(Fig. 2, page 45)*.

Rnd 38: Sc in both loops of each sc around.

Rnds 39-42: Sc in each sc around.

Rnd 43: (Sc2tog, sc in next 4 sc) around: 40 sc.

Rnd 44: (Sc2tog, sc in next 3 sc) around: 32 sc.

Rnd 45: (Sc2tog, sc in next 2 sc) around: 24 sc.

Stuff Head & Body with polyester fiberfill.

Rnd 46: (Sc2tog, sc in next sc) around: 16 sc.

Rnd 47: Sc2tog around: 8 sc.

Rnd 48: Sc in each sc around; slip st in next sc, finish off leaving a long end for sewing.

Thread yarn needle with long end and weave needle through sts on Rnd 48 *(Fig. 5, page 46)*; pull **tightly** to close hole and secure end.

Ears

With Brown, slip st around post of sc 2 rows below Hair on side of Head; ch 3, slip st around post of sc one rnd below; finish off.

Repeat on opposite side of Head.

SKIRT

Rnd 1: With back of Body facing, working in free loops of sc on Rnd 36 *(Fig. 3a, page 45)*, and Head toward you, join Blue with sc in sc at center back; sc in next 4 sc, 2 sc in next sc, (sc in next 5 sc, 2 sc in next sc) around; do **not** join, place marker to indicate beginning of rnd: 56 sc.

Rnd 2: (Sc in next 6 sc, 2 sc in next sc) around: 64 sc.

Rnds 3-8: Sc in each sc around.

Slip st in next sc, finish off.

Rnd 9: With **right** side facing, join Pink with sc in same st as slip st; sc in next 6 sc, 2 sc in next sc, (sc in next 7 sc, 2 sc in next sc) around; join with slip st to first sc, finish off.

ARM (Make 2)

Rnd 1 (Right side)**:** With Brown, ch 2, 4 sc in second ch from hook; do **not** join, place marker to indicate beginning of rnd.

Note: Mark Rnd 1 as **right** side.

Rnd 2: 2 Sc in each sc around: 8 sc.

Rnd 3: (Sc in next sc, 2 sc in next sc) around: 12 sc.

Rnds 4-7: Sc in each sc around.

Slip st in next sc, finish off.

Rnd 8: With **right** side facing, join Blue with sc in same st as slip st; sc in each sc around; join with slip st to first sc.

Rnd 9: Ch 1, sc in same st as joining and in each sc around; do **not** join, place marker to indicate beginning of rnd.

Rnds 10-23: Sc in each sc around.

Slip st in next sc, finish off leaving a long end for sewing.

Stuff Arms with polyester fiberfill, leaving top unstuffed.

LEG (Make 2)
With Blue, ch 4.

Rnd 1 (Right side)**:** Sc in second ch from hook and in next ch, 4 sc in last ch; working in free loops of beginning ch *(Fig. 3b, page 45)*, sc in next ch, 3 sc in next ch; join with slip st to first sc: 10 sc.

Note: Mark Rnd 1 as **right** side.

Rnd 2: Ch 1, sc in same st as joining and in next sc, 2 sc in each of next 4 sc, sc in next 2 sc, 2 sc in each of last 2 sc; join with slip st to first sc: 16 sc.

Rnd 3: Ch 1, sc in same st as joining and in next 2 sc, 2 sc in next sc, (sc in next sc, 2 sc in next sc) 3 times, sc in next 3 sc, 2 sc in next sc, sc in next sc, 2 sc in last sc; join with slip st to Back Loop Only of first sc: 22 sc.

Rnd 4: Ch 1, sc in Back Loop Only of same st as joining and each sc around; join with slip st to **both** loops of first sc.

Rnd 5: Ch 1, sc in same st as joining and in each sc around; join with slip st to first sc.

Rnd 6: Ch 1, sc in same st as joining and in next 2 sc, sc2tog, (sc in next sc, sc2tog) 3 times, sc in each sc around; join with slip st to first sc: 18 sc.

Rnd 7: Ch 1, sc in same st as joining and in next sc, sc2tog 4 times, sc in each sc around; join with slip st to first sc: 14 sc.

Rnd 8: Ch 1, sc in same st as joining and in each sc around; do **not** join, place marker to indicate beginning of rnd.

Rnds 9-13: Sc in each sc around.

Slip st in next sc, finish off.

Rnd 14: With Pink, make a slip knot; holding slip knot on **wrong** side, insert hook in same st as slip st, hook slip knot and pull loop through st, slip st in each sc around; join with slip st to joining slip st, finish off.

Rnd 15: With **right** side facing and working in Back Loops Only of sc on Rnd 13, join Brown with sc in same st as slip st; sc in each sc around; join with slip st to **both** loops of first sc.

Rnd 16: Ch 1, sc in both loops of same st as joining and each sc around; do **not** join, place marker to indicate beginning of rnd.

Rnds 17-28: Sc in each sc around.

Slip st in next sc, finish off leaving a long end for sewing.

Stuff Legs with polyester fiberfill, leaving top unstuffed.

BELT

With Gold, ch 48.

Row 1: Sc in back ridge of second ch from hook and each ch across *(Fig. 1, page 45)*: 47 sc.

Row 2 (Right side)**:** Turn; slip st in first 20 sc, skip next 3 sc, (4 tr, ch 2, 4 tr) in next sc, skip next 3 sc, slip st in each sc across; finish off leaving a long end for sewing.

Note: Mark Row 2 as **right** side.

WRIST BAND (Make 2)

With Pink, ch 12.

Row 1 (Right side)**:** Sc in back ridge of second ch from hook and each ch across: 11 sc.

Note: Mark Row 1 as **right** side.

Rows 2 and 3: Ch 1, turn; sc in each sc across.

Finish off leaving a long end for sewing.

HAIR BOW (Make 2)
Band

With Pink, ch 12.

Row 1 (Right side)**:** Sc in back ridge of second ch from hook and each ch across; finish off leaving a long end for sewing: 11 sc.

Note: Mark Row 1 as **right** side.

With **right** side facing, wrap Band around base of pigtail, sew end of row together.

Bow

With Pink, ch 6.

Row 1 (Right side)**:** Sc in back ridge of second ch from hook and each ch across: 5 sc.

Note: Mark Row 1 as **right** side.

Row 2: Ch 1, turn; sc in each sc across; finish off.

Wrap a 10" (25.5 cm) strand of Pink around center several times and secure yarn; do **not** cut yarn. Sew Bow to Band along seam.

TIARA

With Blue, ch 47; being careful **not** to twist ch; join with slip st in back ridge to form a ring.

Rnd 1 (Right side)**:** Working in back ridge, sc in same ch and in each ch around; join with slip st to first sc: 47 sc.

Note: Mark Rnd 1 as **right** side.

Rnd 2: Slip st in next 19 sc, skip next 3 sc, (4 tr, ch 2, 4 tr) in next sc, skip next 3 sc, slip st in each sc around; join with slip st to joining slip st, finish off.

CAPE

With Pink, ch 22.

Row 1 (Right side)**:** Sc in back ridge of second ch from hook and each ch across: 21 sc.

Note: Mark Row 1 as **right** side.

Rows 2 and 3: Ch 1, turn; sc in each sc across.

Row 4: Ch 1, turn; (sc in next 2 sc, 2 sc in next sc) across: 28 sc.

Rows 5 and 6: Ch 1, turn; sc in each sc across.

Row 7: Ch 1, turn; (sc in next 3 sc, 2 sc in next sc) across: 35 sc.

Rows 8-30: Ch 1, turn; sc in each sc across.

Finish off.

Row 31: With **right** side facing, join Gold with sc in first sc; sc in each sc across.

Rows 32-34: Ch 1, turn; sc in each sc across, finish off.

Trim: With Pink, ch 20 (**first tie made**), with **right** side facing, sc in end of Row 1 and in each row across to last row, skip last row; 3 sc in first sc, sc in each sc across to last sc, 3 sc in last sc; skip first row, sc in end of each row across, ch 20 (**second tie made**), finish off.

ASSEMBLY

Using photo as a guide for placement, with **right** sides of all pieces facing and using long ends:

With **wrong** side of Belt together, sew ends of rows together. Sew Belt to Body.

Thumb: With **right** side facing, join Brown with slip st around post of sc on Rnd 6; ch 3, slip st around post of sc of Rnd 7; finish off.

Repeat for second Arm.

With **wrong** side of Wrist Band together, sew ends of rows together.

Slip one Wrist Band onto each Arm; tack in place.

Flatten Arms; then sew to Rnd 25 on each side of Body.

Flatten Legs; then sew to Rnds 44-48 on each side at bottom of Body.

Tie Cape around neck.

Place Tiara on Head.

CHARLES

CRIMSON DEFENDER

●●○○ EASY

SHOPPING LIST

Yarn (Super Bulky Weight) 🟰**6**
[3.5 ounces, 108 yards
(100 grams, 99 meters) per skein]:

☐ Red - 3 skeins

☐ Ecru - 1 skein

☐ Gold - 1 skein

☐ Black - 1 skein

☐ Gray - 1 skein

Crochet Hook

☐ Size J (6 mm)

or size needed for gauge

Additional Supplies

☐ Safety pins

☐ Yarn needle

☐ 15 mm Safety eyes - 2

☐ Polyester fiberfill - 12 ounces (340 grams)

Finished Size: 15" (38 cm) tall (seated)

GAUGE INFORMATION

10 sc and 12 rows/rnds = 4" (10 cm)

Gauge Swatch: 4" (10 cm) square
With Ecru, ch 11.

Row 1: Sc in second ch from hook
and in each ch across: 10 sc.

Rows 2-12: Ch 1, turn; sc in each sc
across.
Finish off.

STITCH GUIDE

SINGLE CROCHET 2 TOGETHER
 (abbreviated sc2tog)
Pull up a loop in each of next 2 sc,
YO and draw through all 3 loops on
hook **(counts as one sc)**.

HAT

Rnd 1 (Right side)**:** With Red, ch 2,
8 sc in second ch from hook; do
not join, place marker to indicate
beginning of rnd **(see Markers,
page 45)**.

Note: Loop a short piece of yarn
around any stitch to mark Rnd 1 as
right side.

Rnd 2: 2 Sc in each sc around: 16 sc.

Rnd 3: (Sc in next sc, 2 sc in next sc)
around: 24 sc.

Rnd 4: (Sc in next 2 sc, 2 sc in next sc)
around: 32 sc.

Rnd 5: (Sc in next 3 sc, 2 sc in next sc)
around: 40 sc.

Rnd 6: (Sc in next 4 sc, 2 sc in next sc)
around: 48 sc.

Rnds 7-10: Sc in each sc around.

Rnd 11: Sc in each sc around; with
Yellow, slip st in next sc *(Fig. 4,
page 46)*, cut Red.

Rnd 12: Ch 1, sc in same st as slip
st and in each sc around; join with
slip st to first sc.

Rnd 13: Ch 1, sc in same st as joining
and in each sc around; join with
slip st to first sc, finish off.

Rnd 14: With **right** side facing, join
Red with sc in same st as joining *(see
Joining With Sc, page 45)*; sc in each
sc around; join with slip st to first sc.

Rnd 15: Ch 1, sc in same st as joining
and in each sc around; join with
slip st to first sc, finish off leaving a
long end for sewing.

HEAD & BODY

Rnd 1 (Right side)**:** With Ecru and
beginning at top of Head, ch 2, 8 sc
in second ch from hook; do **not** join,
place marker to indicate beginning
of rnd.

Note: Mark Rnd 1 as **right** side.

Rnd 2: 2 Sc in each sc around: 16 sc.

Rnd 3: (Sc in next sc, 2 sc in next sc) around: 24 sc.

Rnd 4: (Sc in next 2 sc, 2 sc in next sc) around: 32 sc.

Rnd 5: (Sc in next 3 sc, 2 sc in next sc) around: 40 sc.

Rnd 6: (Sc in next 4 sc, 2 sc in next sc) around: 48 sc.

Rnds 7-15: Sc in each sc around.

Rnd 16: (Sc in next 4 sc, sc2tog) around: 40 sc.

Rnd 17: Sc in each sc around.

Rnd 18: (Sc in next 3 sc, sc2tog) around: 32 sc.

Rnd 19: (Sc in next 2 sc, sc2tog) around; slip loop from hook onto a safety pin to prevent Head from unraveling while attaching eyes, nose, and Hat: 24 sc.

Attach safety eyes on Rnd 12 of Head, spacing them 6 sc apart.

Using photo, page 9, as a guide for placement and satin stitch *(Fig. 7, page 46)*, add Ecru nose 2 rnds below eyes.

Stuff Head firmly with polyester fiberfill. Using photo, page 19, as a guide for placement, place Hat on Head angling toward the back; using safety pins, pin Hat to Head; remove polyester fiberfill.
Using long end, sew Hat to Head. Remove safety pins.

Rnd 20: Slip loop from safety pin onto crochet hook; (sc2tog, sc in next sc) around: 16 sc.

Rnd 21: (Sc in next sc, 2 sc in next sc) around: 24 sc.

Rnd 22: (Sc in next 2 sc, 2 sc in next sc) around: 32 sc.

Rnd 23: Sc in each sc around; slip st in next sc, finish off.

Rnd 24: With **right** side facing, join Red with sc in same st as slip st; sc in next 2 sc, 2 sc in next sc, (sc in next 3 sc, 2 sc in next sc) around; join with slip st to first sc: 40 sc.

Rnd 25: Ch 1, sc in same st as joining and in each sc around; do **not** join, place marker to indicate beginning of rnd.

Rnd 26: Sc in each sc around.

Rnd 27: (Sc in next 4 sc, 2 sc in next sc) around: 48 sc.

Rnds 28-35: Sc in each sc around.

Rnd 36: Sc in each sc around; slip st in next sc, slip loop from hook onto a safety pin to prevent Body from unraveling while adding accent lines.

Using photo, page 19, as a guide for placement and satin stitch, add Yellow accent lines to front of Body on Rnd 27 working around 3 sc to form top of pocket.

Rnd 37: Slip loop from safety pin onto crochet hook, sc in each sc around.

Rnds 38-42: Sc in each sc around.

Rnd 43: (Sc2tog, sc in next 4 sc) around: 40 sc.

Rnd 44: (Sc2tog, sc in next 3 sc) around: 32 sc.

Rnd 45: (Sc2tog, sc in next 2 sc) around: 24 sc.

Stuff Head & Body with polyester fiberfill.

Rnd 46: (Sc2tog, sc in next sc) around: 16 sc.

Rnd 47: Sc2tog around: 8 sc.

Rnd 48: Sc in each sc around; slip st in next sc, finish off leaving a long end for sewing.

Thread yarn needle with long end and weave needle through sts on Rnd 48 *(Fig. 5, page 46)*; pull **tightly** to close hole and secure end.

ARM (Make 2)

Rnd 1 (Right side)**:** With Black, ch 2, 4 sc in second ch from hook; do **not** join, place marker to indicate beginning of rnd.

Note: Mark Rnd 1 as **right** side.

Rnd 2: 2 Sc in each sc around: 8 sc.

Rnd 3: (Sc in next sc, 2 sc in next sc) around: 12 sc.

Rnds 4-7: Sc in each sc around.

Slip st in next sc, finish off.

Rnd 8: With **right** side facing, join Red with sc in same st as slip st; sc in each sc around; join with slip st to first sc.

Rnd 9: Ch 1, sc in same st as joining and in each sc around; do **not** join, place marker to indicate beginning of rnd.

Rnds 10-23: Sc in each sc around.

Slip st in next sc, finish off leaving a long end for sewing.

Stuff Arms with polyester fiberfill, leaving top unstuffed.

LEG (Make 2)

With Black, ch 4.

Rnd 1 (Right side)**:** Sc in second ch from hook and in next ch, 4 sc in last ch; working in free loops of beginning ch *(Fig. 3b, page 45)*, sc in next ch, 3 sc in next ch; join with slip st to first sc: 10 sc.

Note: Mark Rnd 1 as **right** side.

Rnd 2: Ch 1, sc in same st as joining and in next sc, 2 sc in each of next 4 sc, sc in next 2 sc, 2 sc in each of last 2 sc; join with slip st to first sc: 16 sc.

Rnd 3: Ch 1, sc in same st as joining and in next 2 sc, 2 sc in next sc, (sc in next sc, 2 sc in next sc) 3 times, sc in next 3 sc, 2 sc in next sc, sc in next sc, 2 sc in last sc; join with slip st to Back Loop Only of first sc *(Fig. 2, page 45)*: 22 sc.

Rnd 4: Ch 1, sc in Back Loop Only of same st as joining and each sc around; join with slip st to **both** loops of first sc.

Rnd 5: Ch 1, sc in same st as joining and in each sc around; join with slip st to first sc.

Rnd 6: Ch 1, sc in same st as joining and in next 2 sc, sc2tog, (sc in next sc, sc2tog) 3 times, sc in each sc around; join with slip st to first sc: 18 sc.

Rnd 7: Ch 1, sc in same st as joining and in next sc, sc2tog 4 times, sc in each sc around; join with slip st to first sc: 14 sc.

Rnd 8: Ch 1, sc in same st as joining and in each sc around; join with slip st to first sc.

Rnd 9: Ch 1, sc in same st as joining and in each sc around; do **not** join, place marker to indicate beginning of rnd.

Rnd 10: Sc in each sc around; slip st to Back Loop Only of first sc, finish off.

Rnd 11: With **right** side facing and working in Back Loops Only, join Red with sc in same st as slip st; sc in each sc around; join with slip st to **both** loops of first sc.

Rnd 12: Ch 1, sc in same st as joining and in each sc around; do **not** join, place marker to indicate beginning of rnd.

Rnds 13-28: Sc in each sc around.

Slip st in next sc, finish off leaving a long end for sewing.

Stuff Legs with polyester fiberfill, leaving top unstuffed.

BELT

With Gold, ch 49.

Row 1 (Right side)**:** Dc in back ridge of third ch from hook and each ch across *(Fig. 1, page 45)*; finish off leaving a long end for sewing: 47 dc.

Note: Mark Row 1 as **right** side.

Accessories (Make 3 with Grey and 2 with Black)

Ch 8.

Row 1 (Right side)**:** Sc in back ridge of second ch from hook and each ch across; finish off leaving a long end for sewing.

Note: Mark Row 1 as **right** side.

MASK

With Gold, ch 16.

Row 1 (Right side)**:** Sc in back ridge of second ch from hook and each ch across: 15 sc.

Note: Mark Row 1 as **right** side.

Row 2: Ch 3 (**counts as first dc**), turn; dc in next 3 sc, ch 6, skip next 3 sc, 2 dc in next sc, ch 6, skip next 3 sc, dc in last 4 sc: 10 dc and 12 chs.

Row 3: Ch 1, turn; sc in each dc and in each ch across: 22 sc.

First Tie: Skip end of first row, pull up a loop in end of last 2 rows, YO and draw through all 3 loops on hook, ch 29; finish off.

Second Tie: With **right** side facing, join Gold with slip st in end of Row 1; pull up a loop in end of last 2 rows, YO and draw through all 3 loops on hook, ch 29; finish off.

WRIST BAND (Make 2)

With Gold, ch 14.

Row 1 (Right side)**:** Dc in back ridge of third ch from hook and each ch across; finish off leaving a long end for sewing: 12 dc.

Note: Mark Row 1 as **right** side.

SHIELD
Back

Rnd 1 (Right side)**:** With Black, ch 2, 6 sc in second ch from hook; do **not** join, place marker to indicate beginning of rnd.

Note: Mark Rnd 1 as **right** side.

Rnd 2: 2 Sc in each sc around: 12 sc.

Rnd 3: (Sc in next sc, 2 sc in next sc) around: 18 sc.

Rnd 4: (Sc in next 2 sc, 2 sc in next sc) around: 24 sc.

Rnd 5: (Sc in next 3 sc, 2 sc in next sc) around: 30 sc.

Rnd 6: (Sc in next 4 sc, 2 sc in next sc) around: 36 sc.

Rnd 7: (Sc in next 5 sc, 2 sc in next sc) around: 42 sc.

Rnd 8: (Sc in next 6 sc, 2 sc in next sc) around: 48 sc.

Rnd 9: (Sc in next 7 sc, 2 sc in next sc) around: 54 sc.

Rnd 10: Sc in each sc around.

Rnd 11: (Sc in next 8 sc, 2 sc in next sc) around: 60 sc.

Rnd 12: (Sc in next 9 sc, 2 sc in next sc) around; slip st in next sc, finish off: 66 sc.

Front

Rnd 1 (Right side)**:** With Red, ch 2, 6 sc in second ch from hook; join with slip st to first sc.

Note: Mark Rnd 1 as **right** side.

Rnd 2: Ch 1, 2 sc in same st as joining and in each sc around; join with slip st to first sc, finish off: 12 sc.

Rnd 3: With **right** side facing, join Grey with sc in same st as joining; 2 sc in next sc, (sc in next sc, 2 sc in next sc) around; join with slip st to first sc, finish off: 18 sc.

Rnd 4: With **right** side facing, join Gold with sc in same st as joining; sc in next sc, 2 sc in next sc, (sc in next 2 sc, 2 sc in next sc) around; join with slip st to first sc, do **not** finish off: 24 sc.

Rnd 5: Ch 1, sc in same st as joining and in next 2 sc, 2 sc in next sc, (sc in next 3 sc, 2 sc in next sc) around; join with slip st to first sc, finish off: 30 sc.

Rnd 6: With **right** side facing, join Grey with sc in same st as joining; sc in next 3 sc, 2 sc in next sc, (sc in next 4 sc, 2 sc in next sc) around; join with slip st to first sc, finish off: 36 sc.

Rnd 7: With **right** side facing, join Red with sc in same st as joining; sc in next 4 sc, 2 sc in next sc, (sc in next 5 sc, 2 sc in next sc) around; join with slip st to first sc, do **not** finish off: 42 sc.

Rnd 8: Ch 1, sc in same st as joining and in next 5 sc, 2 sc in next sc, (sc in next 6 sc, 2 sc in next sc) around; join with slip st to first sc, finish off: 48 sc.

Rnd 9: With **right** side facing, join Grey with sc in same st as joining; sc in next 6 sc, 2 sc in next sc, (sc in next 7 sc, 2 sc in next sc) around; join with slip st to first sc, finish off: 54 sc.

Rnd 10: With **right** side facing, join Black with sc in same st as joining; sc in each sc around; join with slip st to first sc; do **not** finish off.

Rnd 11: Ch 1, sc in same st as joining and in next 7 sc, 2 sc in next sc, (sc in next 8 sc, 2 sc in next sc) around; join with slip st to first sc: 60 sc.

Rnd 12: Ch 1, sc in same st as joining and in next 8 sc, 2 sc in next sc, (sc in next 9 sc, 2 sc in next sc) around; join with slip st to first sc: 66 sc.

Joining: With **wrong** sides together and working in **both** loops of **both** layers, slip st in each sc around stuffing Shield with polyester fiberfill before closing; join with slip st to first slip st, finish off.

Strap

With Black and leaving a long end for sewing, ch 5.

Row 1 (Right side)**:** Sc in second ch from hook and in each ch across: 4 sc.

Note: Mark Row 1 as **right** side.

Rows 2-12: Ch 1, turn; sc in each sc.

Finish off leaving long end for sewing.

Using photo, page 25, as a guide for placement, sew ends of Strap to Back.

ASSEMBLY

Using photo as a guide for placement, with **right** sides of all pieces facing and using long ends:

With **wrong** side of Accessories together, sew end of row together.

Alternating colors, slip Accessories onto Belt.

With **wrong** side of Belt together, sew end of row together. Sew Belt to Body moving Accessories in the front.

Thumb: With **right** side facing and using photo as a guide for placement, join Black with slip st around post of sc on Rnd 6; ch 3, slip st around post of sc of Rnd 7; finish off.

Repeat for second Arm.

With **wrong** side of Wrist Band together, sew end of row together.

Sew one Wrist Band onto each Arm.

Flatten Arms; then sew to Rnd 25 on each side of Body.

Flatten Legs; then sew to Rnds 44-48 on each side at bottom of Body.

Tie Cape around neck.

Tie Mask around Head.

Slip Shield onto Arm.

VIOLET

VALIANT HEART

●●○○ EASY

SHOPPING LIST

Yarn (Super Bulky Weight)
[3.5 ounces, 108 yards
(100 grams, 99 meters) per skein**]:**

☐ Ecru - 2 skeins
☐ Purple - 2 skeins
☐ Gold - 2 skeins
☐ Light Pink - 1 skein
☐ Black - 1 skein
☐ Black medium weight - small
  amount (for eyelashes)

Crochet Hook

☐ Size J (6 mm)
  or size needed for gauge

Additional Supplies

☐ Safety pins
☐ Yarn needle
☐ 15 mm Safety eyes - 2
☐ Polyester fiberfill - 12 ounces
  (340 grams)
☐ Light pink crayon (for cheeks)

Finished Size: 15" (38 cm) tall (seated)

GAUGE INFORMATION

10 sc and 12 rows/rnds = 4" (10 cm)

Gauge Swatch: 4" (10 cm) square
With Ecru, ch 11.

Row 1: Sc in second ch from hook
and in each ch across: 10 sc.

Rows 2-12: Ch 1, turn; sc in each sc
across.
Finish off.

STITCH GUIDE

TREBLE CROCHET (abbreviated tr)
YO twice, insert hook in sc indicated,
YO and pull up a loop (4 loops on
hook), (YO and draw through 2 loops
on hook) 3 times.

SINGLE CROCHET 2 TOGETHER
(abbreviated sc2tog)
Pull up a loop in each of next 2 sc,
YO and draw through all 3 loops on
hook (**counts as one sc**).

HAIR

Body

Rnd 1 (Right side): With Gold, ch 2,
8 sc in second ch from hook; do
not join, place marker to indicate
beginning of rnd (**see Markers,
page 45**).

Rnd 2: 2 Sc in each sc around: 16 sc.

Rnd 3: (Sc in next sc, 2 sc in next sc)
around: 24 sc.

Rnd 4: (Sc in next 2 sc, 2 sc in next sc)
around: 32 sc.

Rnd 5: (Sc in next 3 sc, 2 sc in next sc)
around: 40 sc.

Rnd 6: (Sc in next 4 sc, 2 sc in next sc)
around: 48 sc.

Rnds 7-13: Sc in each sc around.

Slip st in next sc, finish off leaving a
long end for sewing.

Strands

Cut 48, 30" (76 cm) strands of Gold.
Fold one strand in half. With **right**
facing and using crochet hook, draw
folded end up through two loops of
sc on Rnd 13 and pull the loose ends
through the folded end; draw the
knot up tightly. Repeat in remaining
sc around Rnd 13.

HEAD & BODY

Rnd 1 (Right side)**:** With Ecru and beginning at top of Head, ch 2, 8 sc in second ch from hook; do **not** join, place marker to indicate beginning of rnd.

Note: Mark Rnd 1 as **right** side.

Rnd 2: 2 Sc in each sc around: 16 sc.

Rnd 3: (Sc in next sc, 2 sc in next sc) around: 24 sc.

Rnd 4: (Sc in next 2 sc, 2 sc in next sc) around: 32 sc.

Rnd 5: (Sc in next 3 sc, 2 sc in next sc) around: 40 sc.

Rnd 6: (Sc in next 4 sc, 2 sc in next sc) around: 48 sc.

Rnds 7-15: Sc in each sc around.

Rnd 16: (Sc in next 4 sc, sc2tog) around: 40 sc.

Rnd 17: Sc in each sc around.

Rnd 18: (Sc in next 3 sc, sc2tog) around: 32 sc.

Rnd 19: (Sc in next 2 sc, sc2tog) around; slip loop from hook onto a safety pin to prevent Head from unraveling while attaching eyes, nose, and Hair: 24 sc.

Attach safety eyes on Rnd 12 of Head, spacing them 6 sc apart.

Using photo, page 35, as a guide for placement and satin stitch *(Fig. 7, page 46)*, add Ecru nose 2 rnds below eyes and using straight stitch *(Fig. 6, page 46)* and medium weight Black, add eyelashes.

Stuff Head firmly with polyester fiberfill.

Place Hair Body on Head angling toward the back. Using safety pins, pin Hair Body to Head; remove polyester fiberfill. Using long end, sew Hair Body to Head. Remove safety pins.

Rnd 20: Slip loop from safety pin onto crochet hook; (sc2tog, sc in next sc) around: 16 sc.

Rnd 21: (Sc in next sc, 2 sc in next sc) around: 24 sc.

Rnd 22: (Sc in next 2 sc, 2 sc in next sc) around: 32 sc.

Rnd 23: Sc in each sc around; slip st in next sc, finish off.

Rnd 24: With **right** side facing, join Black with sc in same st as slip st; sc in next 2 sc, 2 sc in next sc, (sc in next 3 sc, 2 sc in next sc) around; join with slip st to first sc, finish off: 40 sc.

Rnd 25: With **right** side facing, join Pink with sc in same st as joining; sc in each sc around; join with slip st to first sc.

Rnd 26: Ch 1, sc in same st as joining and in each sc around; do **not** join, place marker to indicate beginning of rnd.

Rnd 27: (Sc in next 4 sc, 2 sc in next sc) around: 48 sc.

Rnds 28-36: Sc in each sc around.

Slip st in next sc, finish off.

Rnd 37: With **right** side facing and working in Back Loops Only *(Fig. 2, page 45)*, join Purple with sc in same st as slip st; sc in each sc around; join with slip st to **both** loops of first sc.

Rnd 38: Ch 1, sc in same st as joining and in each sc around; do **not** join, place marker to indicate beginning of rnd.

Rnds 39-42: Sc in each sc around.

Rnd 43: (Sc2tog, sc in next 4 sc) around: 40 sc.

Rnd 44: (Sc2tog, sc in next 3 sc) around: 32 sc.

Rnd 45: (Sc2tog, sc in next 2 sc) around: 24 sc.

Stuff Head & Body with polyester fiberfill.

Rnd 46: (Sc2tog, sc in next sc) around: 16 sc.

Rnd 47: Sc2tog around: 8 sc.

Rnd 48: Sc in each sc around; slip st in next sc, finish off leaving a long end for sewing.

Thread yarn needle with long end and weave needle through sts on Rnd 48 *(Fig. 5, page 46)*; pull **tightly** to close hole and secure end.

SKIRT

Rnd 1: With back of Body facing, working in free loops of sc on Rnd 36 *(Fig. 3a, page 45)*, and Head toward you, join Purple with sc in sc at center back; sc in next 4 sc, 2 sc in next sc, (sc in next 5 sc, 2 sc in next sc) around; do **not** join, place marker to indicate beginning of rnd: 56 sc.

Rnd 2: (Sc in next 6 sc, 2 sc in next sc) around: 64 sc.

Rnds 3-8: Sc in each sc around.

Slip st in next sc, finish off.

Rnd 9: With **right** side facing, join Black with sc in same st as slip st; sc in next 6 sc, 2 sc in next sc, (sc in next 7 sc, 2 sc in next sc) around; join with slip st to first sc, finish off.

ARM (Make 2)

Rnd 1 (Right side): With Black, ch 2, 4 sc in second ch from hook; do **not** join, place marker to indicate beginning of rnd.

Note: Mark Rnd 1 as **right** side.

Rnd 2: 2 Sc in each sc around: 8 sc.

Rnd 3: (Sc in next sc, 2 sc in next sc) around: 12 sc.

Rnds 4-7: Sc in each sc around.

Slip st in Back Loop Only of next sc, finish off.

Rnd 8: With **right** side facing and working in Back Loops Only, join Ecru with sc in same st as slip st; sc in each sc around; join with slip st to **both** loops of first sc.

Rnd 9: Ch 1, sc in same st as joining and in each sc around; do **not** join, place marker to indicate beginning of rnd.

Rnds 10-17: Sc in each sc around.

Slip st in next sc, finish off.

Rnd 18: With **right** side facing, join Pink with sc in same st as slip st; sc in each sc around; join with slip st to first sc.

Rnd 19: Ch 1, sc in same st as joining and in each sc around; do **not** join, place marker to indicate beginning of rnd.

Rnds 20-23: Sc in each sc around.

Slip st in next sc, finish off leaving a long end for sewing.

Stuff Arms with polyester fiberfill, leaving top unstuffed.

LEG (Make 2)

With Black, ch 4.

Rnd 1 (Right side)**:** Sc in second ch from hook and in next ch, 4 sc in last ch; working in free loops of beginning ch *(Fig. 3b, page 45)*, sc in next ch, 3 sc in next ch; join with slip st to first sc: 10 sc.

Note: Mark Rnd 1 as **right** side.

Rnd 2: Ch 1, sc in same st as joining and in next sc, 2 sc in each of next 4 sc, sc in next 2 sc, 2 sc in each of last 2 sc; join with slip st to first sc: 16 sc.

Rnd 3: Ch 1, sc in same st as joining and in next 2 sc, 2 sc in next sc, (sc in next sc, 2 sc in next sc) 3 times, sc in next 3 sc, 2 sc in next sc, sc in next sc, 2 sc in last sc; join with slip st to Back Loop Only of first sc: 22 sc.

Rnd 4: Ch 1, sc in Back Loop Only of same st as joining and each sc around; join with slip st to **both** loops of first sc.

Rnd 5: Ch 1, sc in same st as joining and in each sc around; join with slip st to first sc.

Rnd 6: Ch 1, sc in same st as joining and in next 2 sc, sc2tog, (sc in next sc, sc2tog) 3 times, sc in each sc around; join with slip st to first sc: 18 sc.

Rnd 7: Ch 1, sc in same st as joining and in next sc, sc2tog 4 times, sc in each sc around; join with slip st to first sc: 14 sc.

Rnd 8: Ch 1, sc in same st as joining and in each sc around; join with slip st to first sc.

Rnd 9: Ch 1, sc in same st as joining and in each sc around; do **not** join, place marker to indicate beginning of rnd.

Rnds 10-13: Sc in each sc around.

Slip st in Back Loop Only of next sc, finish off.

Rnd 14: With **right** side facing and working in Back Loops Only, join Ecru with sc in same st as slip st; sc in each sc around; join with slip st to **both** loops of first sc, finish off.

Rnd 15: Ch 1, sc in both loops of same st as joining and in each sc around; do **not** join, place marker to indicate beginning of rnd.

Rnds 16-28: Sc in each sc around.

Slip st in next sc, finish off leaving a long end for sewing.

Stuff Legs with polyester fiberfill, leaving top unstuffed.

HEART

Rnd 1 (Right side)**:** With Purple, ch 3, in third ch from hook work (2 dc, 2 sc, ch 1, dc, ch 1, 2 sc, 2 dc, ch 2, slip st); finish off leaving long end for sewing.

Note: Mark Rnd 1 as **right** side.

BELT

With Black, ch 48.

Row 1 (Right side)**:** Sc in back ridge of second ch from hook and each ch across *(Fig. 1, page 45)*; finish off leaving a long end for sewing.

Note: Mark Row 1 as **right** side.

MASK

With Purple, ch 20.

Row 1 (Right side)**:** 2 Dc in fourth ch from hook, skip next 2 chs, sc in next 2 chs, hdc in next ch, skip next 2 chs, 5 tr in next ch, skip next 2 chs, hdc in next ch, sc in next 2 chs, skip next 2 chs, 3 dc in last ch; finish off: 17 sts.

Note: Mark Rnd 1 as **right** side.

Row 2: With **right** side facing and working in free loops of beginning ch *(Fig. 3b, page 45)*, join Purple with slip st in first ch; slip st in next 7 chs, ch 2, dc in next ch, ch 2, slip st in next 8 chs: 17 sts and 2 ch-2 sps.

Row 3: Ch 1, turn; sc in first 2 slip sts, ch 8, skip next 6 slip sts and next ch-2 sp, sc in next dc, ch 8, skip next ch-2 sp and next 6 slip sts, sc in last 2 slip sts: 5 sc and 16 chs.

Row 4: Ch 3, turn; 2 dc in first sc, skip next sc, slip st in next 6 chs, skip next 2 chs, 5 dc in next sc, skip next 2 chs, slip st in next 6 chs, skip next sc, 3 dc in last sc; finish off.

Ties

With **right** side facing, join Purple with slip st in sc at end of Row 3 on either side; ch 29; finish off.

Repeat on oposite side for second Tie.

ASSEMBLY

Using photo as a guide for placement, with **right** sides of all pieces facing and using long ends:

With **wrong** side of Belt together, sew end of row together. Sew Belt to Body.

Sew Heart to center front of Body.

Thumb: With **right** side facing, join Black with slip st around post of sc on Rnd 6; ch 3, slip st around post of sc of Rnd 7; finish off.

Repeat for second Arm.

Flatten Arms; then sew to Rnd 25 on each side of Body.

Flatten Legs; then sew to Rnds 44-48 on each side at bottom of Body.

Braids

Cut two, 12" (30.5 cm) strands of Purple to secure Braids; set aside.

Beginning at center back and ending off center by 3 sc in the front, gather Hair to each side of Head. Separate first side of Hair into 3 equal sections, braid for approximately 8" (20.5 cm). Wrap Purple strand several times around bottom of braid; secure ends; do **not** cut yarn; tie ends into a bow.

Repeat on opposite side of Head.

Trim ends evenly.

Using light pink crayon, color cheeks.

Tie Mask around Head.

MARVIN MEGA BOY

●●○○ **EASY**

SHOPPING LIST

Yarn (Super Bulky Weight) [6]
[3.5 ounces, 108 yards
(100 grams, 99 meters) per skein]:

- ☐ Dark Blue - 3 skeins
- ☐ Gray - 2 skeins
- ☐ Beige - 1 skein
- ☐ Red - 1 skein
- ☐ White - 1 skein

Crochet Hook

- ☐ Size J (6 mm)
  or size needed for gauge

Additional Supplies

- ☐ Safety pins
- ☐ Yarn needle
- ☐ 15 mm Safety eyes - 2
- ☐ Polyester fiberfill - 12 ounces (340 grams)

Finished Size: 15" (38 cm) tall (seated)

GAUGE INFORMATION

10 sc and 12 rows/rnds = 4" (10 cm)

Gauge Swatch: 4" (10 cm) square
With Beige, ch 11.

Row 1: Sc in second ch from hook
and in each ch across: 10 sc.

Rows 2-12: Ch 1, turn; sc in each sc
across.
Finish off.

STITCH GUIDE

SINGLE CROCHET 2 TOGETHER

(abbreviated sc2tog)

Pull up a loop in each of next 2 sc,
YO and draw through all 3 loops on
hook **(counts as one sc)**.

DOUBLE CROCHET CLUSTER

(uses one dc)

YO, insert hook in next dc, YO and
pull up a loop, YO and draw through
2 loops on hook, YO, insert hook in
same st, YO and pull up a loop, YO
and draw through 2 loops on hook,
YO and draw through all 3 loops on
hook.

HAT

Rnd 1 (Right side)**:** With Dark Blue,
ch 2, 8 sc in second ch from hook;
do **not** join, place marker to indicate
beginning of rnd *(see Markers,
page 45)*.

Note: Loop a short piece of yarn
around any stitch to mark Rnd 1 as
right side.

Rnd 2: 2 Sc in each sc around: 16 sc.

Rnd 3: (Sc in next sc, 2 sc in next sc)
around: 24 sc.

Rnd 4: (Sc in next 2 sc, 2 sc in next sc)
around: 32 sc.

Rnd 5: (Sc in next 3 sc, 2 sc in next sc)
around: 40 sc.

Rnd 6: (Sc in next 4 sc, 2 sc in next sc)
around: 48 sc.

Rnds 7-15: Sc in each sc around.

Slip st in next sc, finish off leaving a
long end for sewing.

Rnd 16: With Red, make a slip knot,
holding slip knot on **wrong** side,
insert hook in same st as slip st, hook
slip knot and pull loop through st;
slip st in each sc around; join with
slip st to first slip st, finish off.

Using photo, page 37, as a guide for
placement and satin stitch *(Fig. 7,
page 46)*, add White triangle to Hat.

HEAD & BODY

Rnd 1 (Right side)**:** With Beige and beginning at top of Head, ch 2, 8 sc in second ch from hook; do **not** join, place marker to indicate beginning of round.

Note: Mark Rnd 1 as **right** side.

Rnd 2: 2 Sc in each sc around: 16 sc.

Rnd 3: (Sc in next sc, 2 sc in next sc) around: 24 sc.

Rnd 4: (Sc in next 2 sc, 2 sc in next sc) around: 32 sc.

Rnd 5: (Sc in next 3 sc, 2 sc in next sc) around: 40 sc.

Rnd 6: (Sc in next 4 sc, 2 sc in next sc) around: 48 sc.

Rnds 7-15: Sc in each sc around.

Rnd 16: (Sc in next 4 sc, sc2tog) around: 40 sc.

Rnd 17: Sc in each sc around.

Rnd 18: (Sc in next 3 sc, sc2tog) around: 32 sc.

Rnd 19: (Sc in next 2 sc, sc2tog) around; slip loop from hook onto a safety pin to prevent Head from unraveling while attaching eyes, nose, and Hat: 24 sc.

Attach safety eyes on Rnd 12 of Head, spacing them 6 sc apart.

Using photo, page 38, as a guide for placement and satin stitch, add Beige nose 2 rnds below eyes.

Stuff Head firmly with polyester fiberfill. Using photo as a guide for placement, place Hat on Head angling toward the back; using safety pins, pin Hat to Head; remove polyester fiberfill.
Using long end, sew Hat to Head. Remove safety pins.

Rnd 20: Slip loop from safety pin onto crochet hook; (sc2tog, sc in next sc) around: 16 sc.

Rnd 21: (Sc in next sc, 2 sc in next sc) around: 24 sc.

Rnd 22: (Sc in next 2 sc, 2 sc in next sc) around: 32 sc.

Rnd 23: Sc in each sc around; slip st in next sc, finish off.

Rnd 24: With **right** side facing, join Grey with sc in same st as slip st *(see Joining With Sc, page 45)*; (sc in next 3 sc, 2 sc in next sc) around; join with slip st to first sc: 40 sc.

Rnd 25: Ch 1, sc in same st as joining and in each sc around; do **not** join, place marker to indicate beginning of rnd.

Rnd 26: Sc in each sc around.

Rnd 27: (Sc in next 4 sc, 2 sc in next sc) around: 48 sc.

Rnds 28-36: Sc in each sc around.

Slip st in next sc, finish off.

Using photo as a guide for placement and satin stitch, add White triangle to center front of Body.

Rnd 37: With **right** side facing, join Dark Blue with sc in same st as slip st; sc in each sc around; join with slip st to first sc.

Rnd 38: Ch 1, sc in same st as joining and in each sc around; do **not** join, place marker to indicate beginning of rnd.

Rnds 39-42: Sc in each sc around.

Rnd 43: (Sc2tog, sc in next 4 sc) around: 40 sc.

Rnd 44: (Sc2tog, sc in next 3 sc) around: 32 sc.

Rnd 45: (Sc2tog, sc in next 2 sc) around: 24 sc.

Stuff Head & Body with polyester fiberfill.

Rnd 46: (Sc2tog, sc in next sc) around: 16 sc.

Rnd 47: Sc2tog around: 8 sc.

Rnd 48: Sc in each sc around; slip st in next sc, finish off leaving a long end for sewing.

Thread yarn needle with long end and weave needle through sts on Rnd 48 *(Fig. 5, page 46)*; pull **tightly** to close hole and secure end.

ARM (Make 2)

Rnd 1 (Right side)**:** With Beige, ch 2, 4 sc in second ch from hook; do **not** join, place marker to indicate beginning of rnd.

Note: Mark Rnd 1 as **right** side.

Rnd 2: 2 Sc in each sc around: 8 sc.

Rnd 3: (Sc in next sc, 2 sc in next sc) around: 12 sc.

Rnds 4-7: Sc in each sc around.

Slip st in next sc, finish off.

Rnd 8: With **right** side facing, join Grey with sc in same st as slip st; sc in each sc around; join with slip st to first sc.

Rnd 9: Ch 1, sc in same st as joining and in each sc around; do **not** join, place marker to indicate beginning of rnd.

Rnds 10-23: Sc in each sc around.

Slip st in next sc, finish off leaving a long end for sewing.

Stuff Arms with polyester fiberfill, leaving top unstuffed.

LEG (Make 2)

With Red, ch 4.

Rnd 1 (Right side)**:** Sc in second ch from hook and in next ch, 4 sc in last ch; working in free loops of beginning ch *(Fig. 3b, page 45)*, sc in next ch, 3 sc in next ch; join with slip st to first sc: 10 sc.

Note: Mark Rnd 1 as **right** side.

Rnd 2: Ch 1, sc in same st as joining and in next sc, 2 sc in each of next 4 sc, sc in next 2 sc, 2 sc in each of last 2 sc; join with slip st to first sc: 16 sc.

Rnd 3: Ch 1, sc in same st as joining and in next 2 sc, 2 sc in next sc, (sc in next sc, 2 sc in next sc) 3 times, sc in next 3 sc, 2 sc in next sc, sc in next sc, 2 sc in last sc; join with slip st to Back Loop Only of first sc *(Fig. 2, page 45)*: 22 sc.

Rnd 4: Ch 1, sc in Back Loop Only of same st as joining and each sc around; join with slip st to **both** loops of first sc.

Rnd 5: Ch 1, sc in same st as joining and in each sc around; join with slip st to first sc.

Rnd 6: Ch 1, sc in same st as joining and in next 2 sc, sc2tog (sc in next sc, sc2tog) 3 times, sc in each sc around; join with slip st to first sc: 18 sc.

Rnd 7: Ch 1, sc in same st as joining and in next sc, sc2tog 4 times, sc in each sc around; join with slip st to first sc: 14 sc.

Rnd 8: Ch 1, sc in same st as joining and in each sc around; join with slip st to first sc.

Rnd 9: Ch 1, sc in same st as joining and in each sc around; do **not** join, place marker to indicate beginning of rnd.

Rnds 10-13: Sc in each sc around.

Slip st in Back Loop Only of next sc, finish off.

Rnd 14: With **right** side facing and working in Back Loops Only, join Dark Blue with sc in same st as slip st; sc in each sc around; join with slip st to **both** loops of first sc.

Rnd 15: Ch 1, sc in same st as joining and in each sc around; do **not** join, place marker to indicate beginning of rnd.

Rnds 16-28: Sc in each sc around.

Slip st in next sc, finish off leaving a long end for sewing.

Stuff Legs with polyester fiberfill, leaving top unstuffed.

BELT

With Red, ch 48.

Row 1 (Right side)**:** Sc in back ridge of second ch from hook and each ch across *(Fig. 1, page 45)*; finish off leaving a long end for sewing: 47 sc.

Note: Mark Row 1 as **right** side.

CAPE

With Dark Blue, ch 22.

Row 1 (Right side)**:** Sc in back ridge of second ch from hook and each ch across: 21 sc.

Note: Mark Row 1 as **right** side.

Rows 2 and 3: Ch 1, turn; sc in each sc across.

Row 4: Ch 1, turn; (sc in next 2 sc, 2 sc in next sc) across: 28 sc.

Rows 5 and 6: Ch 1, turn; sc in each sc across.

Row 7: Ch 1, turn; (sc in next 3 sc, 2 sc in next sc) across: 35 sc.

Rows 8-16: Ch 1, turn; sc in each sc across.

Finish off.

Row 17: With **right** side facing, join White with sc in first sc; sc in each sc across.

Row 18: Ch 1, turn; sc in each sc across; finish off.

Row 19: With **right** side facing, join Red with sc in first sc; sc in each sc across.

Row 20: Ch 1, turn; sc in each sc across; finish off.

Rows 21-36: Repeat Rows 17-20, 4 times.

Trim: With Dark Blue, ch 20 (**first tie made**); with **right** side facing, sc in end of Row 1 and in each row across to last row, skip last row; 3 sc in first sc, sc in each sc across to last sc, 3 sc in last sc; skip first row, sc in end of each row across, ch 20 (**second tie made**); finish off.

MASK

With Dark Blue, ch 17.

Row 1 (Right side)**:** Dc in back ridge of third ch from hook and each ch acros (**3 skipped chs count as first dc**): 15 dc.

Note: Mark Row 1 as **right** side.

Row 2: Ch 3 (**does not count as a st, now and throughout**), turn; sc in first dc, hdc in next dc, dc in next dc, ch 7, skip next 4 dc, work dc Cluster in next dc, ch 7, skip next 4 dc, dc in next dc, hdc in next dc, sc in last dc: 7 sts and 2 ch-7 sps.

Row 3: Ch 3, turn; (slip st, ch 1, sc) in first sc, hdc in next hdc, dc in next dc, (5 dc, 2 hdc, sc) in next ch-7 sp, 3 dc in next st, (sc, 2 hdc, 5 dc) in next ch-7 sp, dc in next dc, hdc in next hdc, sc in last sc.

First Tie: Ch 29; finish off.

Second Tie: With **right** side facing, join Dark Blue with slip st in first sc on Row 3; ch 29; finish off.

ASSEMBLY

Using photos as a guide for placement, with **right** sides of all pieces facing and using long ends:

With **wrong** side of Belt together, sew end of row together. Sew Belt to Body.

Thumb: With **right** side facing, join Beige with slip st around post of sc on Rnd 6; ch 3, slip st around post of sc of Rnd 7; finish off.

Repeat for second Arm.

Flatten Arms; then sew to Rnd 25 on each side of Body.

Flatten Legs; then sew to Rnds 44-48 on each side at bottom of Body.

Tie Cape around neck.

Tie Mask around Head.

General Instructions

ABBREVIATIONS

ch(s)	chain(s)
cm	centimeters
dc	double crochet(s)
hdc	half double crochet(s)
mm	millimeters
Rnd(s)	Round(s)
sc	single crochet(s)
sc2tog	single crochet 2 together
sp(s)	space(s)
st(s)	stitch(es)
tr	treble crochet(s)
YO	yarn over

SYMBOLS & TERMS

★ — work instructions following ★ as many **more** times as indicated in addition to the first time.

( ) or [ ] — work enclosed instructions **as many** times as specified by the number immediately following **or** work all enclosed instructions in the stitch or space indicated **or** contains explanatory remarks.

colon (:) — the number(s) given after a colon at the end of a row or round denote(s) the number of stitches or spaces you should have on that row or round.

GAUGE

Exact gauge is **essential** for proper size. Before beginning your project, make the sample swatch given in the individual instructions in the yarn and hook specified. After completing the swatch, measure it, counting your stitches and rows carefully. If your swatch is larger or smaller than specified, **make another, changing hook size to get the correct gauge.** Keep trying until you find the size hook that will give you the specified gauge.

CROCHET HOOKS																	
U.S.	B-1	C-2	D-3	E-4	F-5	G-6	7	H-8	I-9	J-10	K-10½	L-11	M/N-13	N/P-15	P/Q	Q	S
Metric - mm	2.25	2.75	3.25	3.5	3.75	4	4.5	5	5.5	6	6.5	8	9	10	15	16	19

CROCHET TERMINOLOGY	
UNITED STATES	INTERNATIONAL
slip stitch (slip st)	= single crochet (sc)
single crochet (sc)	= double crochet (dc)
half double crochet (hdc)	= half treble crochet (htr)
double crochet (dc)	= treble crochet (tr)
treble crochet (tr)	= double treble crochet (dtr)
double treble crochet (dtr)	= triple treble crochet (ttr)
triple treble crochet (tr tr)	= quadruple treble crochet (qtr)
skip	= miss

■□□□ BEGINNER	Projects for first-time crocheters using basic stitches. Minimal shaping.
■■□□ EASY	Projects using yarn with basic stitches, repetitive stitch patterns, simple color changes, and simple shaping and finishing.
■■■□ INTERMEDIATE	Projects using a variety of techniques, such as basic lace patterns or color patterns, mid-level shaping and finishing.
■■■■ EXPERIENCED	Projects with intricate stitch patterns, techniques and dimension, such as non-repeating patterns, multi-color techniques, fine threads, small hooks, detailed shaping and refined finishing.

MARKERS

Markers are used to help distinguish the beginning of each round being worked. Place a 2" (5 cm) scrap piece of yarn before the first stitch of each round, moving the marker after each round is complete.

JOINING WITH SC

When instructed to join with sc, begin with a slip knot on hook. Insert hook in stitch or space indicated, YO and pull up a loop, YO and draw through both loops on hook.

BACK RIDGE OF A CHAIN

Work only in loops indicated by arrows (*Fig. 1*).

Fig. 1

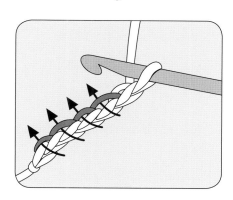

BACK LOOPS ONLY

Work only in loop(s) indicated by arrow (*Fig. 2*).

Fig. 2

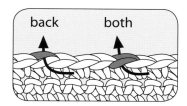

FREE LOOPS

After working in Back Loops Only on a round, there will be a ridge of unused loops. These are called the free loops. Later, when instructed to work in the free loops of the same row or round, work in these loops (*Fig. 3a*).

When instructed to work in free loops of a chain, work in loop indicated by arrow (*Fig. 3b*).

Fig. 3a

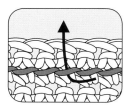

Fig. 3b

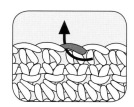

Yarn Weight Symbol & Names	LACE 0	SUPER FINE 1	FINE 2	LIGHT 3	MEDIUM 4	BULKY 5	SUPER BULKY 6	JUMBO 7
Type of Yarns in Category	Fingering, size 10 crochet thread	Sock, Fingering, Baby	Sport, Baby	DK, Light Worsted	Worsted, Afghan, Aran	Chunky, Craft, Rug	Super Bulky, Roving	Jumbo, Roving
Crochet Gauge* Ranges in Single Crochet to 4" (10 cm)	32-42 sts**	21-32 sts	16-20 sts	12-17 sts	11-14 sts	8-11 sts	6-9 sts	5 sts and fewer
Advised Hook Size Range	Steel*** 6 to 8, Regular hook B-1	B-1 to E-4	E-4 to 7	7 to I-9	I-9 to K-10½	K-10½ to M/N-13	M/N-13 to Q	Q and larger

*GUIDELINES ONLY: The chart above reflects the most commonly used gauges and hook sizes for specific yarn categories.

** Lace weight yarns are usually crocheted with larger hooks to create lacy openwork patterns. Accordingly, a gauge range is difficult to determine. Always follow the gauge stated in your pattern.

*** Steel crochet hooks are sized differently from regular hooks–the higher the number, the smaller the hook, which is the reverse of regular hook sizing.

CHANGING COLORS

Drop yarn, insert hook in first stitch, with new yarn, YO and draw through stitch and loop on hook *(Fig. 4)*.

Fig. 4

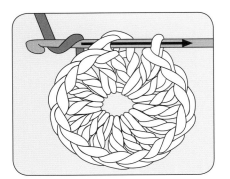

EMBROIDERY STITCHES
STRAIGHT STITCH

Straight stitch is just what the name implies, a single, straight stitch. Come up at 1 and go down at 2 *(Fig. 6)*.

Fig. 6

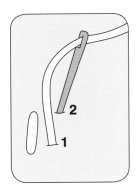

SATIN STITCH

Satin Stitch is a series of straight stitches worked side by side that come out of and go into the same stitch *(Fig. 7)*. Come up at odd numbers and go down at even numbers.

Fig. 7

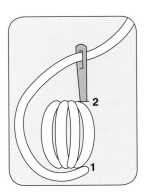

WEAVE THRU STITCHES

Weave yarn end through the stitches *(Fig. 5)* and gather to close.

Fig. 5

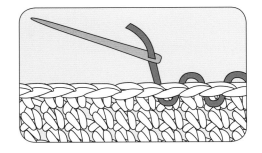

yarn Information

The projects in this book were made using Bernat® Softee® Chunky™, a Super Bulky Weight yarn. Any brand of the specified yarn weight may be used. It is best to refer to the yardage/meters when determining how many balls or skeins to purchase. Remember, to arrive at the finished size, it is the GAUGE/TENSION that is important, not the brand of yarn.

For your convenience, listed below are the specific colors used to create our photography models. Because yarn manufacturers make frequent changes in their product lines, you may sometimes find it necessary to use a substitute yarn or to search for the discontinued product at alternate suppliers (locally or online).

ANTON/ATOMIC FLYER
Orange - #28630 Pumpkin
White - #28005 White
Brown - #28011 Soft Taupe
Black - #28040 Black
Gold - #28607 Glowing Gold

CHARLES/CRIMSON DEFENDER
Red - #28705 Berry Red
Ecru - #28008 Natural
Gold - #28607 Glowing Gold
Black - #28040 Black
Gray - #28046 Gray Heather

MARVIN/MEGA BOY
Dark Blue - #28134 Royal Blue
Gray - #28046 Gray Heather
Biege - #28021 Linen
Red - #28705 Berry Red
White - #28005 White

PATTY/POWERFUL PRINCESS
Blue - #28742 Ultra Blue
Brown - #28011 Soft Taupe
Pink - #28416 Hot Pink
Dark Brown - #28013 Dark Taupe
Gold - #28607 Glowing Gold

VIOLET/VALIANT HEART
Ecru - #28008 Natural
Purple - #28323 Dark Mauve
Gold - #28607 Glowing Gold
Light Pink - #28418 Baby Pink
Black - #28040 Black

We have made every effort to ensure that these instructions are accurate and complete. We cannot, however, be responsible for human error, typographical mistakes, or variations in individual work.

Production Team: Instructional/Technical Writer - Lois J. Long; Senior Graphic Artist - Lora Puls; Graphic Artist - Kytanna McFarlin; Photo Stylist - Lori Wenger; and Photographer - Jason Masters.

MEET
KRiSTi SiMPSON

Kristi Simpson enjoys designing cute baby gifts that mothers will love using. "There's just something special about having a handmade gift," she says. "It's personal and unique."

Inspired by her love of yarn, she creates crochet and knit patterns with a fresh and modern touch. The mother of five became hooked on crochet after teaching herself so she could help her daughter make a scarf from a "learn to crochet" kit that was a gift.

"I loved it from the beginning," she says. "I was amazed that I could take a string of yarn and create something so useful and pretty! Needless to say, I never stopped!"

Look for other Leisure Arts books featuring Kristi's designs at www.leisurearts.com/meet-the-designers/kristi-simpson.html.

Visit kristisimpson.net or find her on Ravelry, Facebook, and Pinterest.